dr.a.g.

by bookthefilm

dr.a.g. | dræg | *folk etymology*

[acronym for dressed as girl] from the early days of the theatre when men played both the male and female roles. One was either 'dressed as girl' (dr.a.g.) or 'dressed as boy' (dr.a.b.)

dr.a.g. | dræg | *étymologie folklorique*

[acronyme de Dressed As Girl, habillé en fille] datant des débuts du théâtre, lorsque les hommes jouaient à la fois les rôles de femme et d'homme. Ils étaient soit « dr.ag. » (dressed as girl – habillés en femme) soit « dr.a.b » (dressed as boy – habillés en homme).

dr.a.g. | dræg | *etimologia popolare*

[acronimo di dressed as girl, vestito da donna] risale agli inizi della storia del teatro, quando gli uomini recitavano sia i ruoli maschili che quelli femminili. Ci si poteva abbigliare "dr.a.g." (dressed as girl – vestito da donna) o "dr.a.b." (dressed as boy – vestito da uomo).

dr.a.g. | dræg | *volksetomologie*

[letterwoord voor 'dressed as girl'] afkomstig uit de vroege dagen van het theater toen mannen zowel de mannelijke als vrouwelijke rollen voor hun rekening namen. Ze waren toen 'dressed as girl' (dr.a.g.) of 'dressed as boy' (dr.a.b.)

TECTUM
PUBLISHERS

Introduction

In the early days of theatre, male actors played both the male and female roles. They were either dr.a.g. (dressed as girl) or dr.a.b. (dressed as boy).

We've Come A Long Way, Baby!

Drag has become a diverse form of expression that challenges, entertains, and educates by pushing boundaries, while embracing beauty, comedy and glamour. The performers in this book are evidence of that diversity, captured by some of the top photographers working in the world today.

All the performers and photographers in this book have graciously donated their work to make this book possible. What started as a small independent film fundraiser has grown into the beautiful book you now hold.

We give great thanks to all of them, but especially to one well-loved performer of the Las Vegas strip. So enthusiastic about the Drag Book Project, he called and cajoled his fellow entertainers to send in photographs and led us through recommendations and connections to others.

Thanks to these connections with drag royalty such as Frank Marino, Eddie Edwards, Randy Roberts, Mr. Kenneth Blake, Chad Michaels and Elaine Lancaster, we earned the credibility to approach others, including drag icons Jackie Beat, Charles Busch, Lady Bunny, Joey Arias, our amazing

'Marilyn Monroe centerspread' Jimmy James, Miss Coco Peru and the legendary Jim Bailey, who closes our book.

To have collected the work of all these wonderful performers and photographers in one book is something we're very proud of, but we acknowledge it never would have been possible without our 'connector angel', Mr. Larry Edwards.

Larry's positive energy, spirit and talent are in large part what this book is celebrating, and so we felt it only right that he start the show.

You can turn the page now...

Introduction

Au début du théâtre, les acteurs jouaient à la fois les rôles d'hommes et de femmes. Ils étaient soit « dr.a.g. » (dressed as girl – habillés en femme) soit « dr.a.b. » (dressed as boy - habillés en homme).

We've Come A Long Way, Baby! On vient de loin...

Se travestir est devenu un mode d'expression différent qui défie, amuse et éduque en repoussant les frontières et en incarnant la beauté, la comédie et le glamour. Les artistes présents dans ce livre sont la preuve vivante de cette diversité, capturée par les plus grands photographes du moment.

Tous les artistes et tous les photographes ont fait don de leur travail afin que ce projet voie le jour. Ce qui avait commencé comme une petite collecte de fonds pour films indépendants a grandi pour devenir le livre que vous tenez entre vos mains.

Nous les remercions tous chaleureusement, mais surtout l'artiste bien-aimé du spectacle de Las Vegas qui, transporté par le Drag Book Project, a su amadouer ses confrères afin qu'ils nous envoient leurs photos. Il nous a donné des recommandations et nous a mis en contact avec d'autres artistes.

C'est ainsi que nous vous présentons les 'hommes en drag' les plus célèbres dont Frank Marino, Eddie Edwards, Randy Roberts, Mr. Kenneth Blake, Chad Michaels et Elaine Lancaster, et que nous avons eu suffisamment de crédibilité pour en approcher d'autres, dont les icônes Jackie Beat, Charles Busch, Lady Bunny, Joey Arias, notre incroyable « Marilyn Monroe en double page » Jimmy James, Miss Coco Peru et le légendaire Jim Bailey, qui clôt notre ouvrage.

Nous sommes très fiers d'avoir pu rassembler le travail de ces magnifiques artistes et photographes dans un livre mais nous savons que rien n'aurait été possible sans notre « ange connecteur », M. Larry Edwards.

L'énergie positive de Larry, son esprit et son talent, voilà en somme ce qui est célébré dans ce livre. Il est donc normal qu'il ouvre le show.

Vous pouvez tourner la page maintenant...

© 2012 Tectum Publishers NV
Naussaustraat 40-42
2000 Antwerp
Belgium
info@tectum.be
+ 32 3 226 66 73
www.tectum.be

ISBN: 978-946158-02-90
WD: 2012/9021/01
(155)

Author/Editor:
Christopher Logan
Design: Mamio Marais
Translations: Carole Touati (French), Birgit Krols (Dutch)

Printed in China

Introduzione

Fino al XXVII secolo nella storia del teatro erano solo gli attori uomini a recitare sia i ruoli maschili che quelli femminili. Potevano essere infatti "dr.a.g.", (dressed as girl - vestiti da donna) o "dr.a.b." (dressed as boy - vestiti da uomo).

We've Come A Long Way, Baby! Ne abbiamo fatta di strada!

Il Drag è diventato una forma di espressione molto varia , che sfida, diverte e educa premendo ai confini, e incarnando allo stesso tempo bellezza, commedia e fascino. Gli artisti in questo libro, immortalati da alcuni dei migliori fotografi del momento, sono i testimoni di questa varietà.

Tutti hanno generosamente donato il loro lavoro per rendere possibile la realizzazione di questo volume. Ciò che era cominciato come un piccolo progetto di raccolta fondi per un film indipendente si è trasformato nel sorprendente libro che sfoglierete.

Desideriamo ringraziare tutti loro sentitamente, e in particolare un artista molto amato della Las Vegas strip. Così entusiasta del progetto Drag Book da contattare e convincere i suoi colleghi a inviarci le loro fotografie, mettendoci in contatto con loro e guidandoci in questo mondo con preziosi consigli .

Grazie ai contatti con i più famosi artisti Drag come Frank Marino, Eddie Edwards, Randy Roberts, Kenneth Blake, Chad Michaels ed Elaine Lancaster, ci siamo guadagnati la credibilità necessaria per avvicinare icone drag come Jackie Beat, Charles Busch, Lady Bunny, Joey Arias, la nostra fantastica "Marilyn Monroe" delle pagine centrali, Jimmy James, Miss Coco Peru e il leggendario Jim Bailey, che chiude il libro.

Raccogliere il lavoro di tutti questi meravigliosi artisti e fotografi in un unico libro ci da grande soddisfazione, ma riconosciamo anche che tutto questo non sarebbe stato possibile senza il nostro "angelico contatto", Larry Edwards.

L' incredibile energia e lo spirito positivo di Larry, il suo talento, sono in gran parte ciò che viene celebrato in questo libro, perciò ci è sembrato giusto che fosse lui ad aprire lo show.

Ora è il momento di girare pagina...

Inleiding

In de vroege dagen van het theater werden zowel mannelijke als vrouwelijke rollen ingevuld door mannelijke acteurs. Ze waren dr.a.g. ('dressed as girl' of 'gekleed als meisje') ofwel dr.a.b. ('dressed as boy' of 'gekleed als jongen').

We've Come A Long Way, Baby! We komen van ver, schatje!

Drag is uitgegroeid tot een ruime expressievorm die uitdaagt, amuseert en bijbrengt door grenzen te verleggen en schoonheid, komedie en glamour te omarmen. De artiesten in dit boek, gezien door de lens van enkele van 's werelds beste fotografen, leveren het bewijs van de diversiteit van deze kunstvorm.

Alle artiesten en fotografen zijn zo vriendelijk geweest om hun werk gratis af te staan om dit boek mogelijk te maken. Wat het licht zag als een kleine, onafhankelijke inzamelactie voor de onafhankelijke film, is uitgegroeid tot het prachtige boek dat u nu in handen heeft.

We willen iedereen hartelijk bedanken, maar vooral één zeer geliefde artiest van de Las Vegas strip. Zo enthousiast was hij over het Drag-project, dat hij prompt collega's begon op te bellen om hen te overhalen foto's in te sturen, en ons aanbevelingen en connecties bezorgde naar anderen toe.

Onze contacten met drag royalty zoals Frank Marino, Eddie Edwards, Randy Roberts, Mr. Kenneth Blake, Chad Michaels en Elaine Lancaster, verleenden ons de nodige geloofwaardigheid om nog anderen te contacteren, inclusief drag iconen zoals Jackie Beat, Charles Busch, Lady Bunny, Joey Arias, onze onwaarschijnlijke 'Marilyn Monroe centerspread' Jimmy James, Miss Coco Peru en de legendarische Jim Bailey, die het boek afsluit.

We zijn erg trots op het feit dat we erin geslaagd zijn het werk van al deze getalenteerde artiesten en fotografen te verzamelen in één boek, maar we zijn ons er ook goed van bewust dat dit nooit mogelijk zou zijn geweest zonder onze 'contactengel', Mr. Larry Edwards.

Larry's positieve energie, spirit en talent zijn grotendeels wat dit boek wil vieren, en dus vonden we het niet meer dan normaal dat hij de show mag beginnen.

U mag de bladzijde nu omslaan...

Larry Edwards

LAS VEGAS, NEVADA

photography **Ninon Nguyen**

Krystal Something-Something

BROOKLYN, NEW YORK ~ photography **Diana Sonis**

Joan Jullian

STEKENE, BELGIUM

photography **Foto Rudesign**

SAL-E

CHICAGO, ILLINOIS

photography **Anthony Meade**

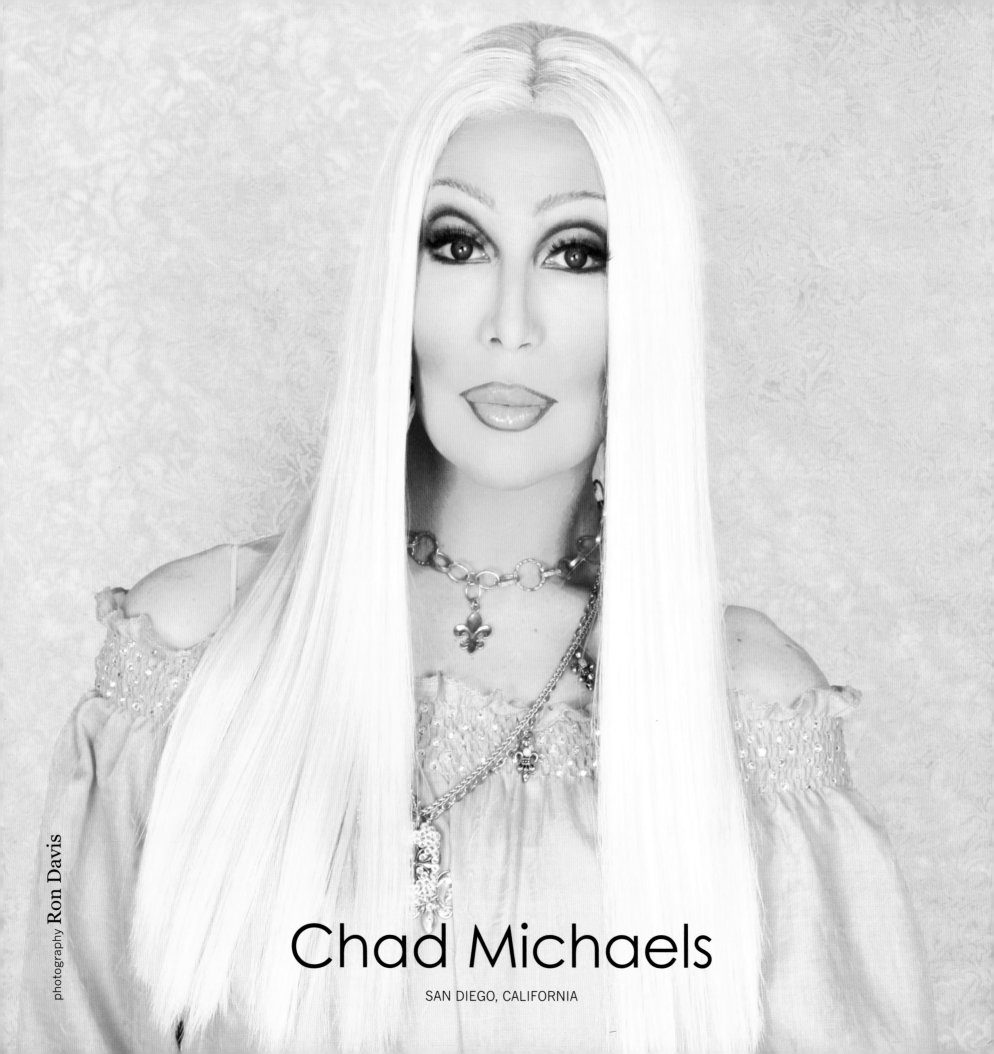

Chad Michaels

SAN DIEGO, CALIFORNIA

Sherry Vine

NEW YORK, NEW YORK ~ photography Anna Patin

ToyBocks Studios
www.lashesnlipstick.com.au

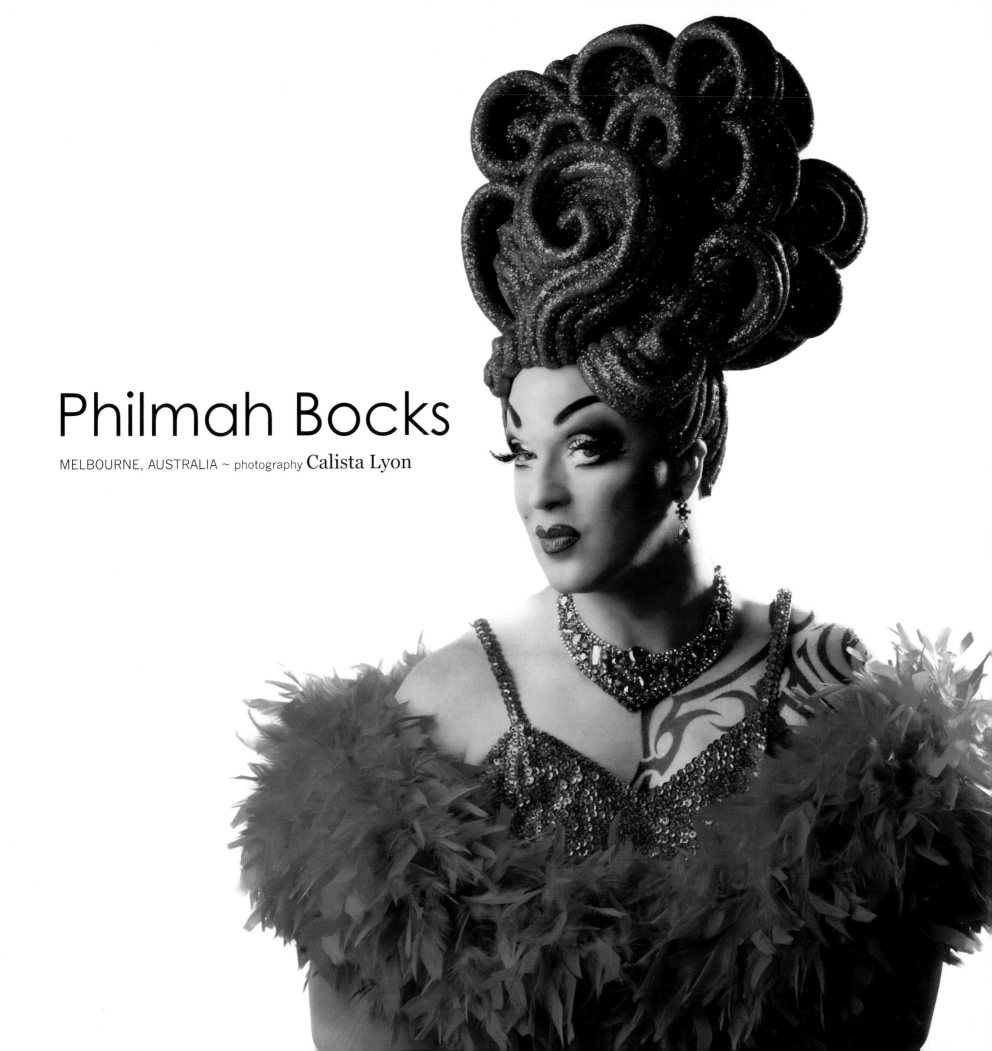

Philmah Bocks

MELBOURNE, AUSTRALIA ~ photography Calista Lyon

Jaylene Tyme

VANCOUVER, BRITISH COLUMBIA

photography Nicholas Jang

"It's amazing what a man can accomplish...

« C'est incroyable ce qu'un homme peut accomplir... quand il porte la robe qu'il faut. »
"È incredibile cosa può fare un uomo... se indossa il vestito giusto."
"Het is ongelooflijk wat een man kan verwezenlijken... wanneer hij de juiste jurk draagt."

when he's wearing the right dress"

Frank Marino

LAS VEGAS, NEVADA

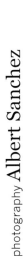

Dixie Longate

MOBILE, ALABAMA

photography **Bradford Rogne**

SHEQUIDA

NEW YORK, NEW YORK

Jeffree Star

OUTER SPACE

photography **Austin Young**

Glitz Glam

SAN DIEGO, CALIFORNIA

photography **Jesse Thomas Greika**

Roxxxy
Andrews

ORLANDO, FLORIDA ~ photography Kristofer Reynolds

Mr.
Kenneth Blake

LAS VEGAS, NEVADA

photography **David Wagner**

SWEETIE

NEW YORK, NEW YORK

photography **Michael Wakefield**

KRISTOFER REYNOLDS photography

ORLANDO, FLORIDA ~ www.kristoferreynolds.com

"Clothes may not make the man...

« L'habit ne fait pas le moine... mais il fait indéniablement la femme. »
"L'abito non farà il monaco... ma decisamente fa la donna."
"Kleren mogen de man dan niet maken... ze maken wel degelijk de vrouw."

but they definitely make the woman."

Eddie Edwards

LAS VEGAS, NEVADA ~ photography **Tim Pacton**

Erica Andrews

SAN ANTONIO, TEXAS ~ photography **Kristofer Reynolds**

Gigi Monroe

LOS ANGELES, CALIFORNIA

photography **Dan Gore**

Carlos Bieletto

MEXICO CITY, MEXICO

photography Alex Villalobos

Randy Roberts

KEY WEST, FLORIDA

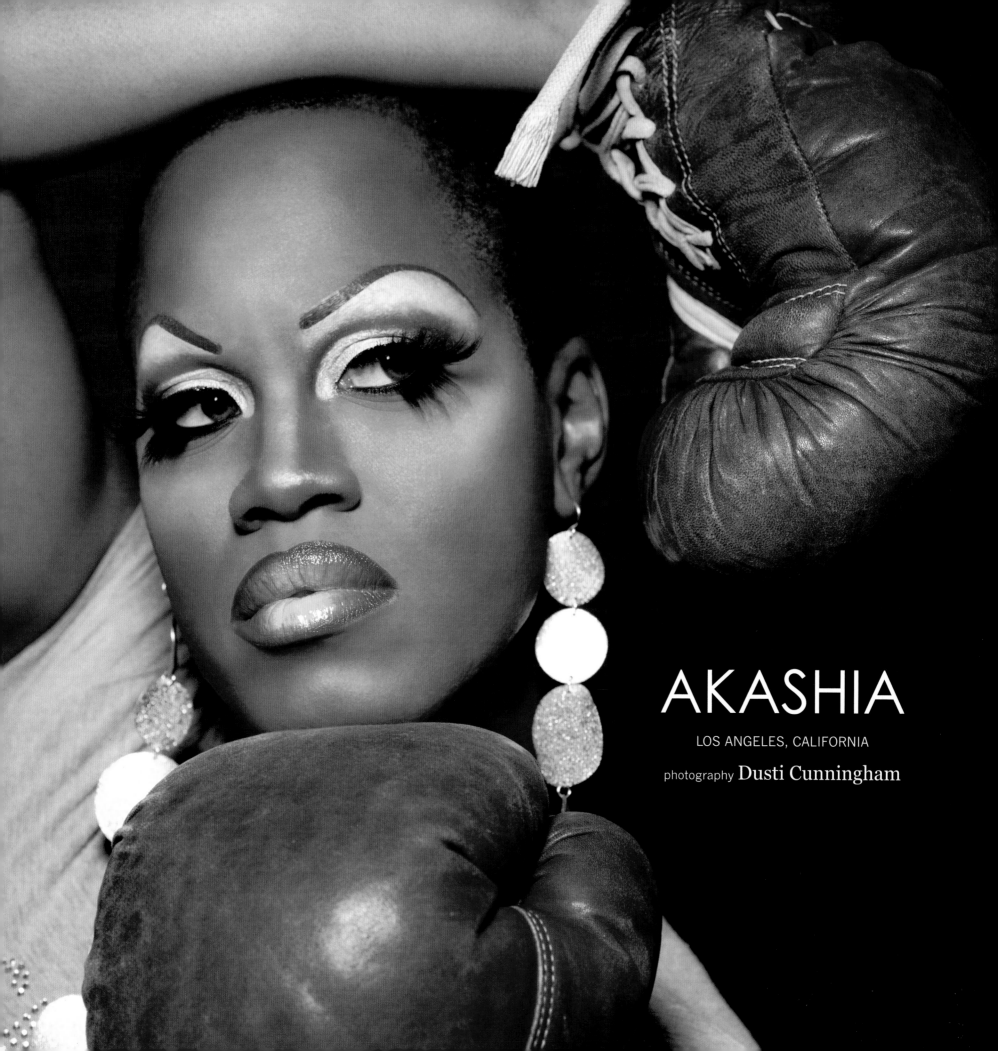

AKASHIA

LOS ANGELES, CALIFORNIA

photography **Dusti Cunningham**

Disco Dollie

SAN DIEGO, CALIFORNIA

photography Peter Palladino

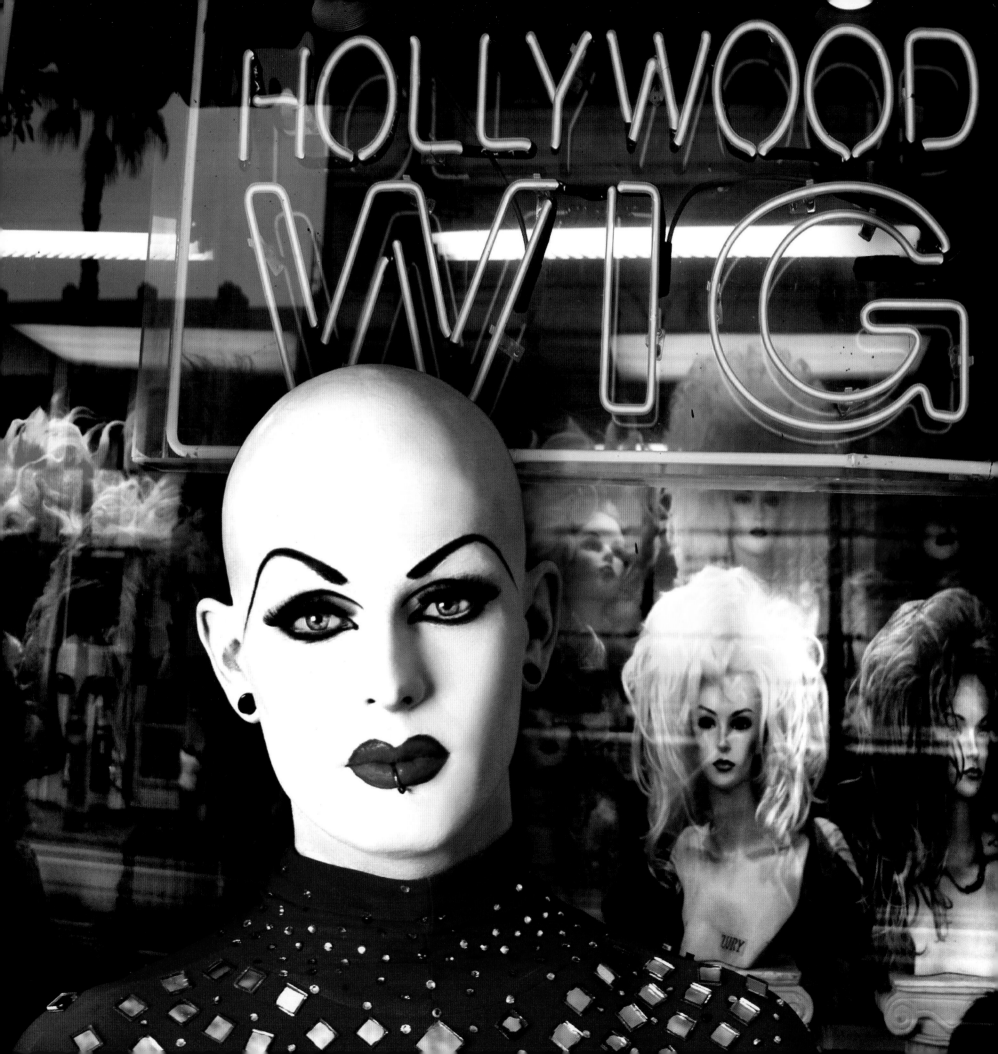

Christopher
Peterson

TORONTO, ONTARIO

photography **David Hawe**

photography Bob Bowden

ANN BROWN photography

KANSAS CITY, MISSOURI ~ www.annbrownphotography.com

make up & styling **Andy Chambers**

"Imitation...

« L'imitation... est la forme de flatterie la plus glamour qui soit. »
"L'imitazione... è la forma più affascinante di adulazione."
"Imitatie... is de meest glamoureuze vorm van vleierij."

is the most glamorous form of flattery"

Jimmy James has retired his Marilyn Monroe impersonation and moved on to a successful music career.

Jimmy James a mis à la retraite son imitation de Marilyn Monroe pour embrasser une belle carrière musicale.

Jimmy James non interpreta più Marilyn Monroe ed è passato a una carriera musicale di successo.

Jimmy James hield zijn Marilyn Monroe imitatie voor bekeken om zich volledig te wijden aan een succesvolle muziekcarrière.

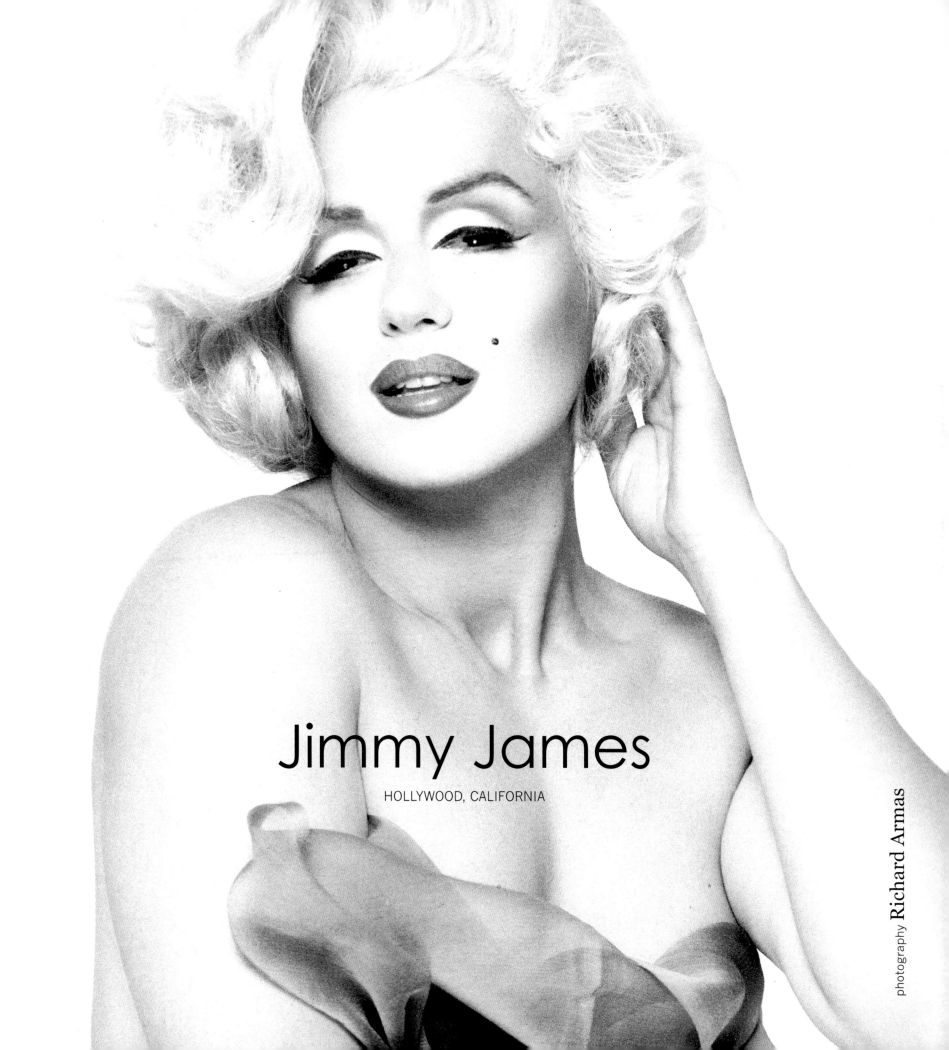

Jimmy James

HOLLYWOOD, CALIFORNIA

photography **Richard Armas**

MIKE RUIZ photography

NEW YORK, NEW YORK ~ www.mikeruiz.com

TAMMIE BROWN, SCHURON D. WOMACK, KEVIN WHILEY, CHAD MICHAELS, MIKE RUIZ, SHANNEL, CHRISTIAN GREENIA, NOSEPH TRINH, VENUS D'LITE

"Dr.a.g. isn't what you wear or who you are...

« Dr.a.g ce n'est ni ce que vous portez ni qui vous êtes... c'est comment vous portez qui vous êtes. »
"Dr.a.g. non è ciò che indossi o chi sei... è come indossi ciò che sei."
"Dr.a.g. is niet wat je draagt of wie je bent. Het is hoe je draagt wie je bent."

it's how you wear who you are"

Nina Flowers

DENVER, COLORADO ~ photography Norman Dillon

Shari Turner

CLEVELAND, OHIO

Blind 7 Photography

Hedda Lettuce

NEW YORK, NEW YORK ~ photography **Manu Rodriguez/ManuFoto**

Miss Cotton

VANCOUVER, BRITISH COLUMBIA

photography **Nicholas Jang**

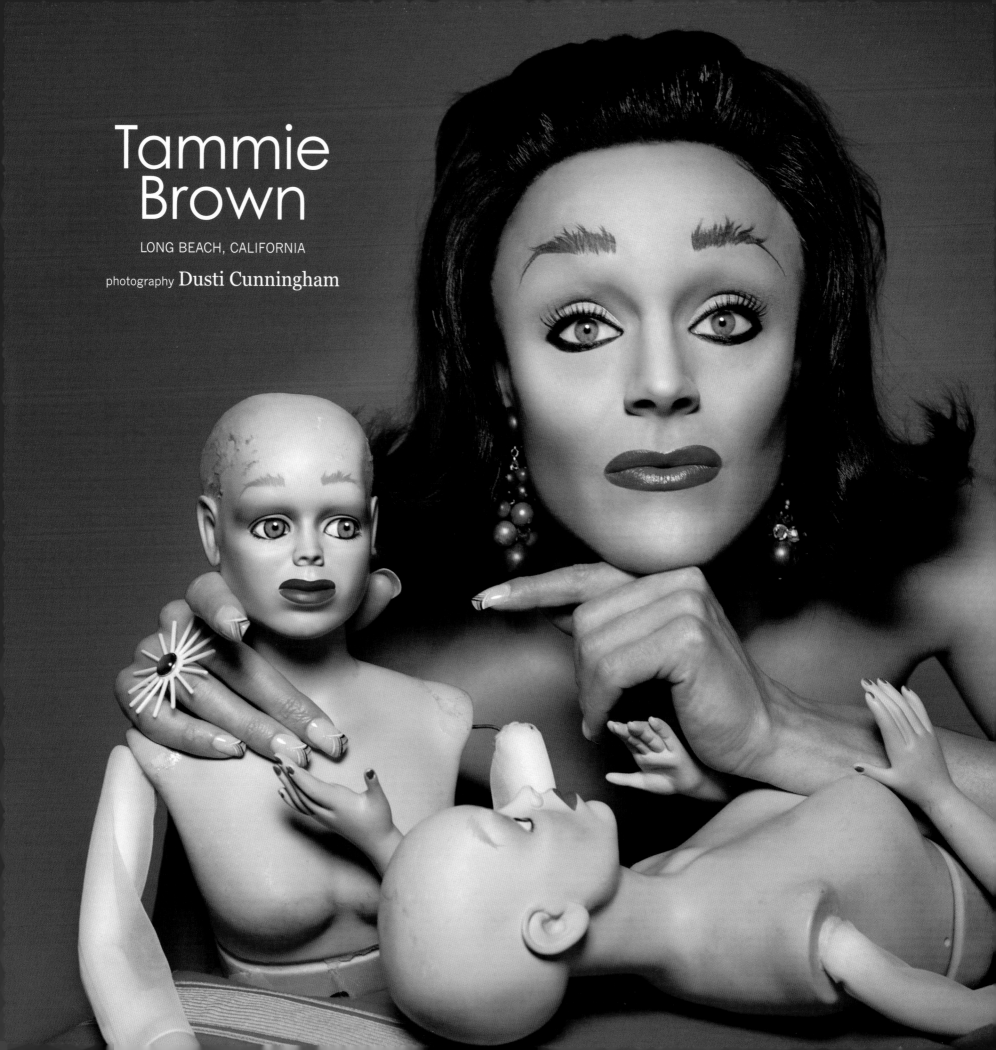

Tammie
Brown

LONG BEACH, CALIFORNIA

photography **Dusti Cunningham**

BeBe Zahara Benet

CAMAROON, WEST AFRICA ~ photography **Terry Hastings**

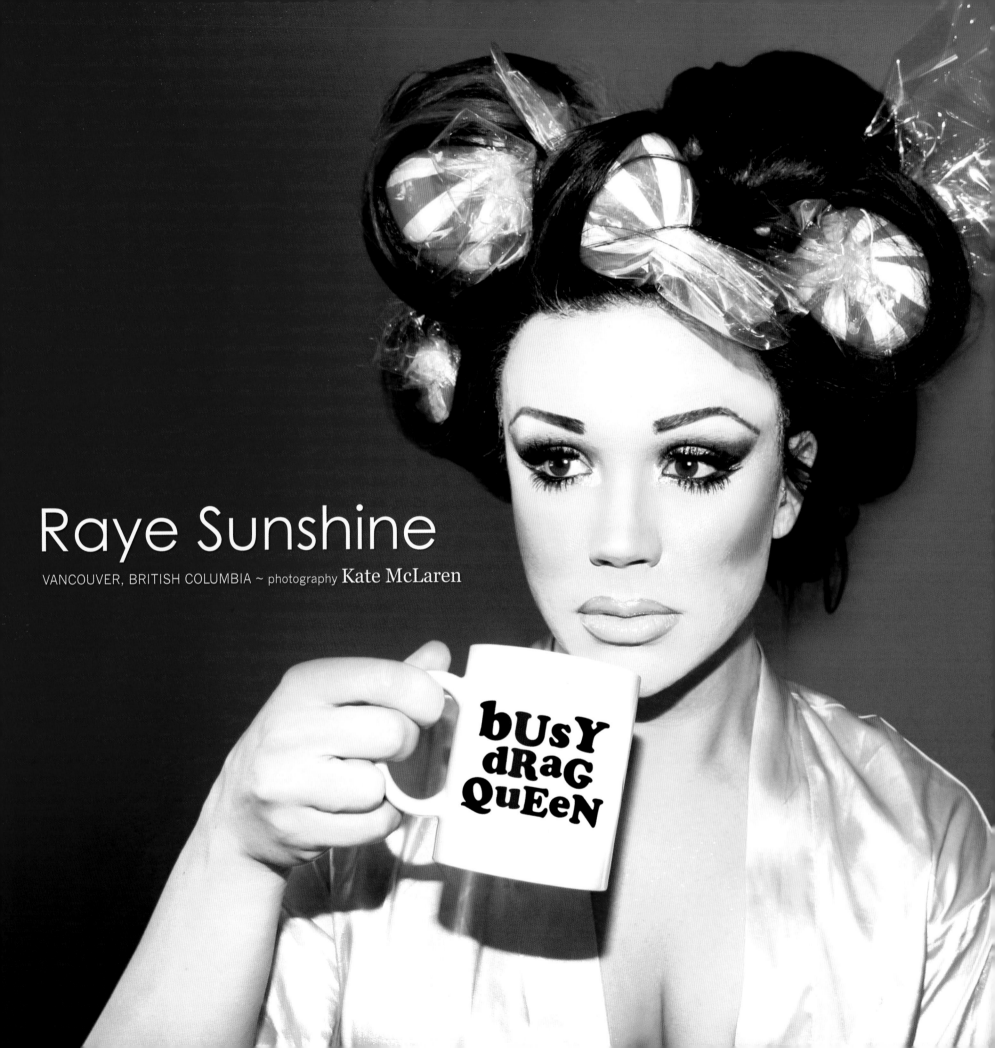

Raye Sunshine

VANCOUVER, BRITISH COLUMBIA ~ photography **Kate McLaren**

bUsY dRaG QuEeN

Guy Labrecque

VANCOUVER, BRITISH COLUMBIA ~ photography **Sergei Bachlakov**

JOSE A GUZMAN COLON photography

SAN FRANCISCO, CALIFORNIA ~ www.joseaguzmancolon.com

PEACHES CHRIST

"Inside every great man...

is a great woman"

Joey Arias

NEW YORK, NEW YORK ~ photography Krys Fox

Vegas
Van Cartier

VANCOUVER, BRITISH COLUMBIA

photography **Nicholas Jang**

EDIE

LAS VEGAS, NEVADA ~ photography **Arslan Gusengadzhiev**

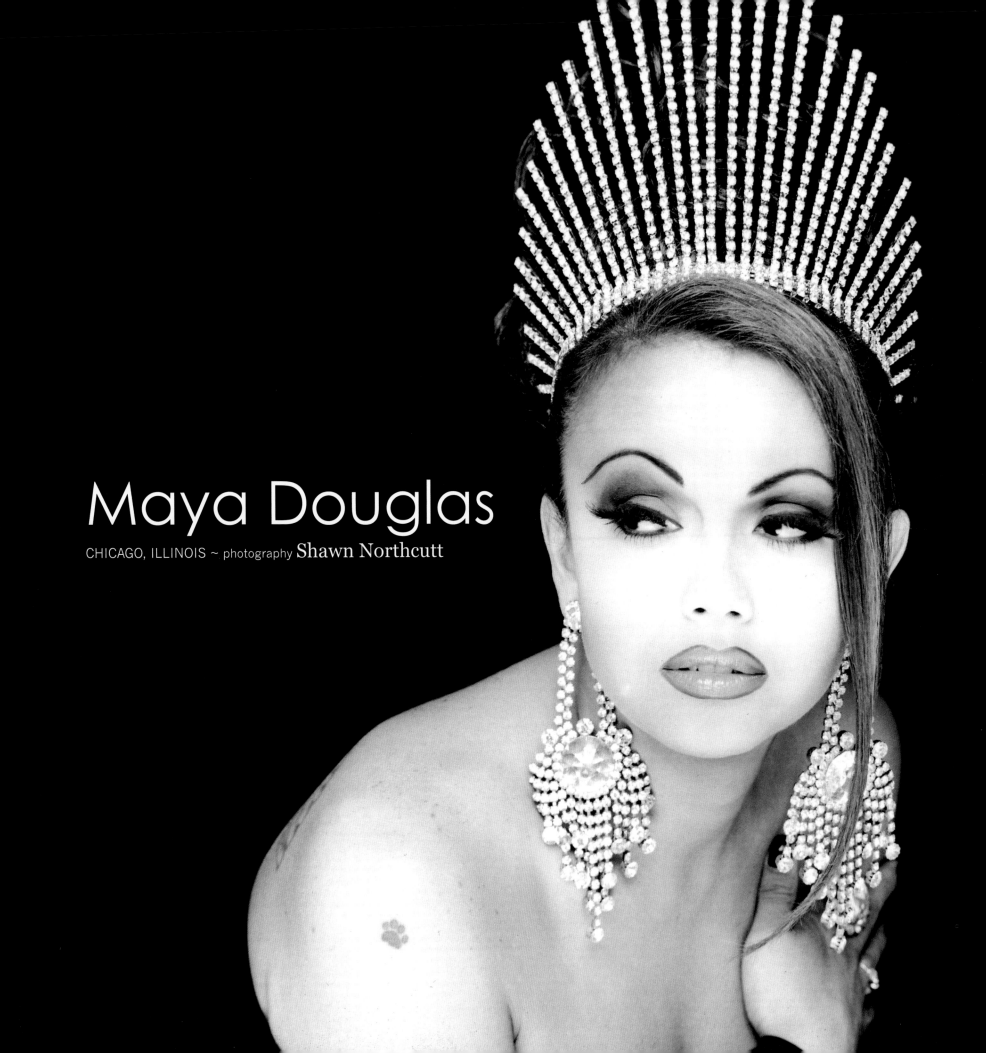

Maya Douglas

CHICAGO, ILLINOIS ~ photography **Shawn Northcutt**

SHANNEL

LOS ANGELES, CALIFORNIA ~ photography William Dick, WDPhotoInc

Miss Barbie-Q

LOS ANGELES, CALIFORNIA

ONGINA

LOS ANGELES, CALIFORNIA

photography **Norman Dillon**

RAJA

LOS ANGELES, CALIFORNIA ~ photography **Austin Young**

AUSTIN YOUNG photography

LOS ANGELES, CALIFORNIA ~ www.austinyoung.com

"There's something different about that girl...

« Il y a quelque chose de différent chez cette fille… ce sera une star ! »
"Quella ragazza ha qualcosa di particolare… diventerà una star!"
"Er is iets speciaals aan dit meisje… ze gaat een ster worden!"

she's going to be a star!"

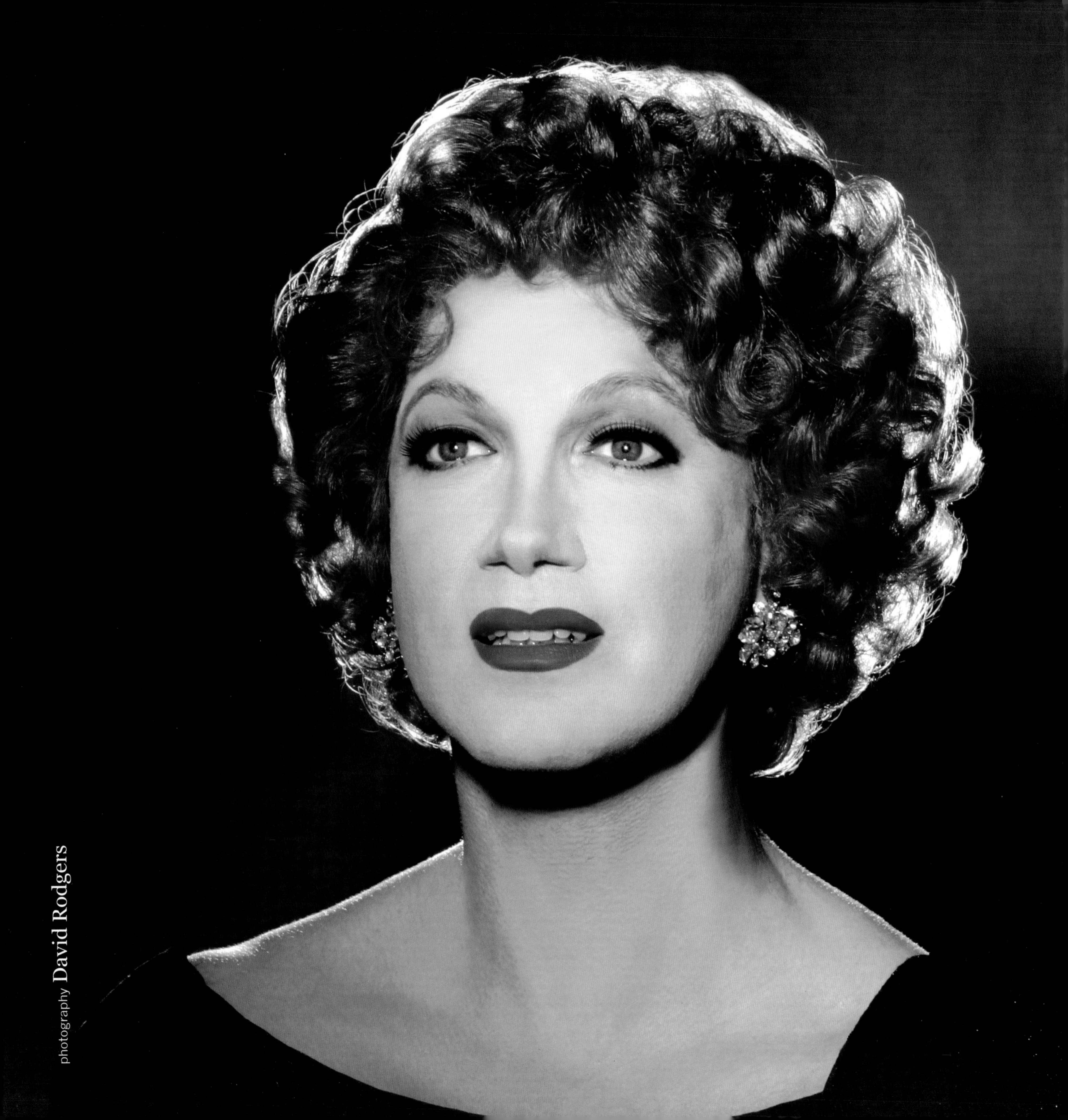
photography David Rodgers

Charles Busch

NEW YORK, NEW YORK

photography **Douglas Levere**

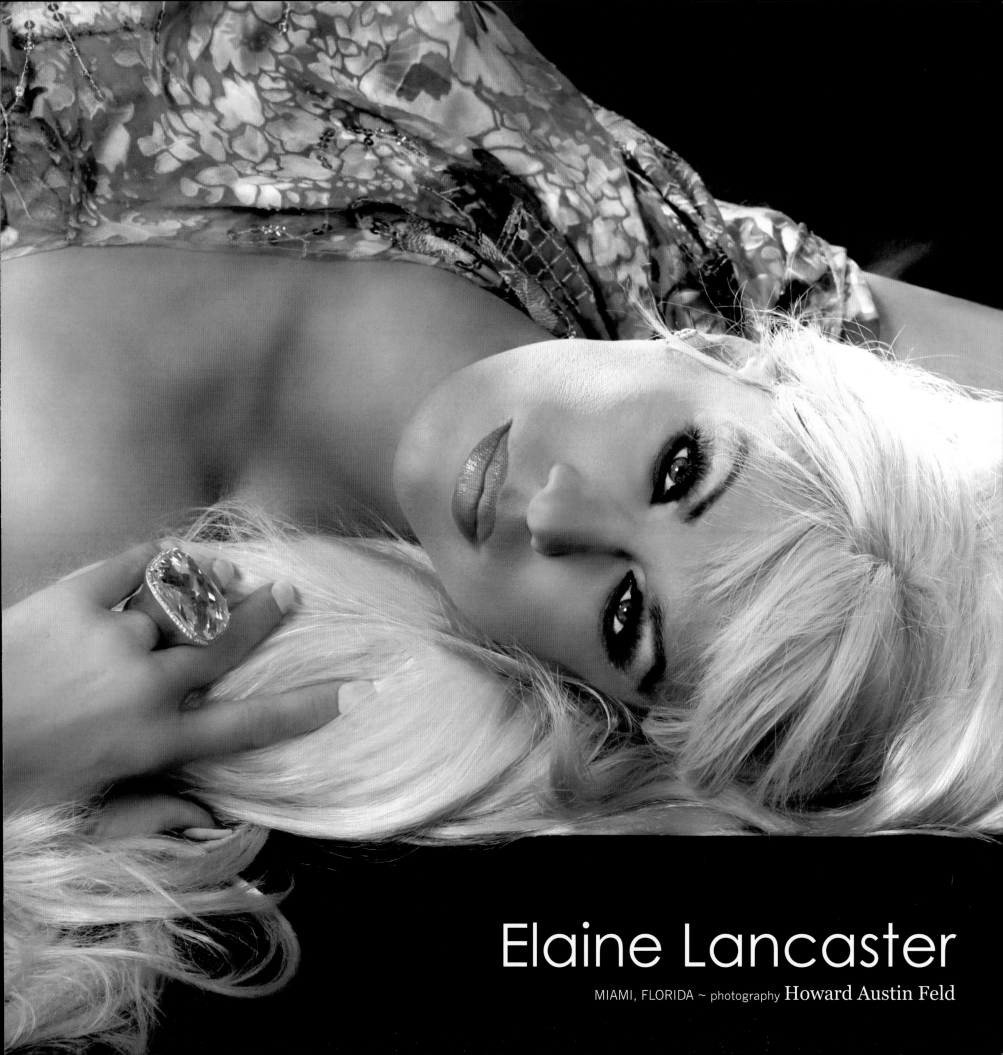

Elaine Lancaster

MIAMI, FLORIDA ~ photography Howard Austin Feld

Miss Coco Peru

LOS ANGELES, CALIFORNIA ~ photography Peter Palladino

MADO

MONTREAL, QUEBEC

photography Jose A Guzman Colon

Jackie Beat

LOS ANGELES, CALIFORNIA ~ photography **Austin Young**

Lady Bunny

NEW YORK, NEW YORK ~ photography Peter Palladino

PETER PALLADINO photography

LOS ANGELES, CALIFORNIA ~ www.palladinodenphotography.com

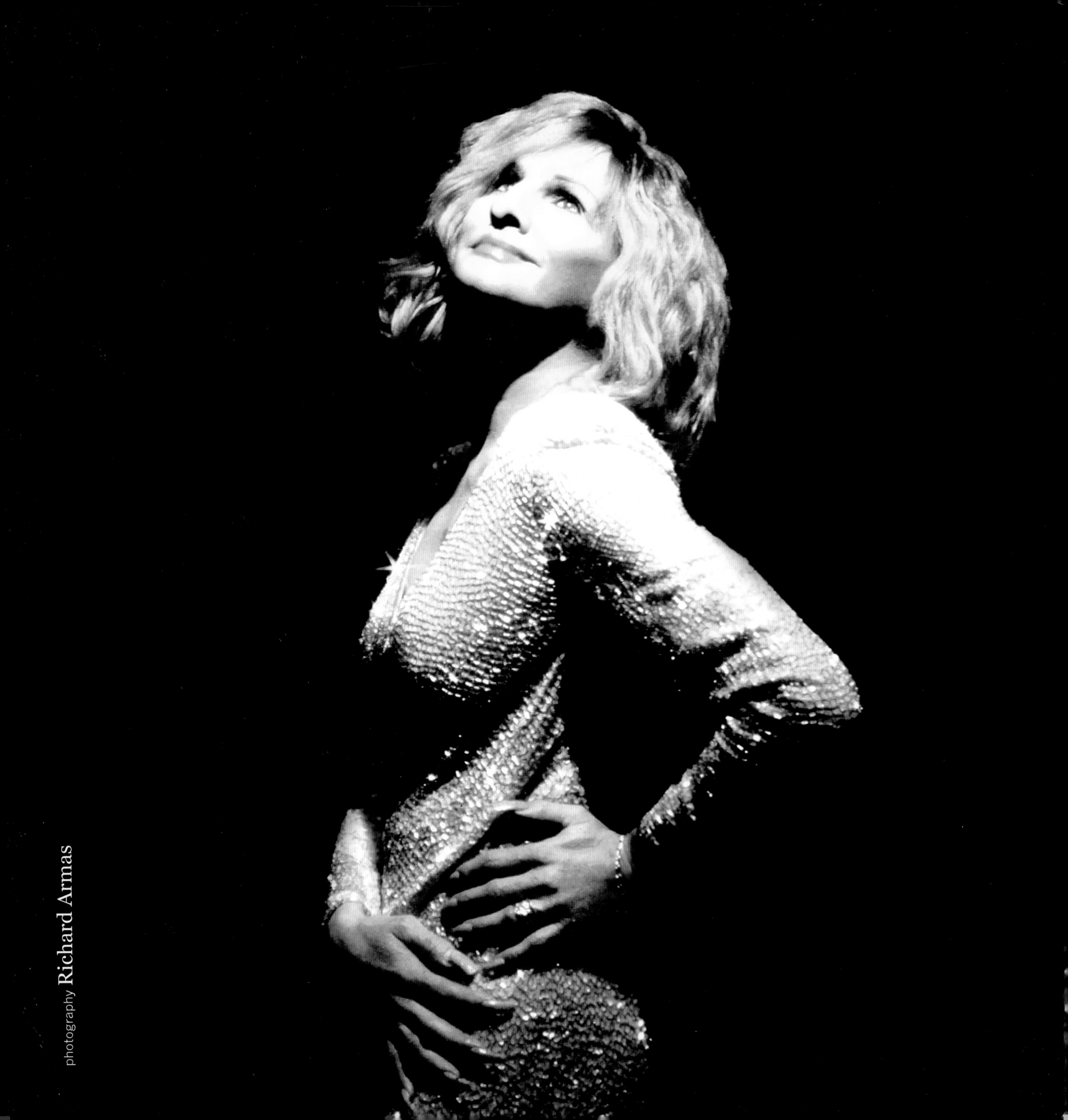

photography Richard Armas

Jim Bailey

photography Peter Palladino

Our final page features the legendary Mr. Jim Bailey. Jim has performed for the British Royal Family, at Carnegie Hall, and has turned in over 70 television and film appearances (including my favorite, The Carol Burnett Show).

We are very honoured to have him close our book.

We hope you enjoyed seeing the world of drag through our eyes. It was an honour to show it to you.

The book dr.a.g. was put together to raise funds for independent film productions. All of the featured performers and photographers graciously donated their work, talent and images, and we are extremely grateful.

We hope you will take a moment to look up these performers and photographers to see where and when you can next see them in action. In the internet age, all it takes is a quick online search to uncover their world.

For information on our upcoming book and film productions, please visit our website.

La dernière page est consacrée au légendaire M. Jim Bailey. Jim s'est produit au Carnegie Hall et devant la famille royale britannique, il compte plus de soixante-dix apparitions à la télévision et dans des films (dont mon préféré The Carol Burnett Show) ; c'est un honneur pour nous de vous le présenter.

Nous espérons que vous avez aimé découvrir le monde des 'hommes en drag' à travers nos yeux. Nous sommes enchantés de l'avoir partagé avec vous.

Le livre dr.a.g a vu le jour pour récolter des fonds pour la production de films indépendants. Tous les artistes et photographes présentés ont fait don de leur travail, de leur talent, de leurs images ; nous en sommes extrêmement reconnaissants.

Nous espérons que vous prendrez un moment pour en savoir plus sur ces artistes et photographes afin de voir où et quand ils se produiront. À l'ère d'Internet, un simple clic permet de découvrir le monde entier.

Pour de plus amples informations concernant notre prochain livre et la production de films, veuillez consultez notre site Web.

Le ultime pagine ritraggono il leggendario Jim Bailey. Jim ha recitato per la famiglia reale inglese a Carnegie Hall e conta più di 70 apparizioni televisive e cinematografiche (incluso il mio show preferito, The Carol Burnett Show).

Siamo davvero molto onorati di esserci potuti avvalere della sua collaborazione.

Ci auguriamo che questo variopinto e affascinante viaggio fotografico nel mondo Drag attraverso i nostri occhi vi sia piaciuto. Per noi è stato un onore mostrarvelo.

Il libro dr.a.g. è stato realizzato per raccogliere fondi per la produzione di film indipendenti. Tutti gli artisti e i fotografi presentati ci hanno cortesemente donato il loro lavoro, il loro talento e le loro straordinarie immagini, pertanto desideriamo esprimergli la nostra più profonda gratitudine.

Qualora aveste qualche minuto per approfondire la conoscenza di questi artisti e fotografi e scoprire dove e quando li potrete vedere all'opera, nell'era di internet una veloce ricerca online vi aprirà le porte verso questo nuovo mondo.

Per ulteriori informazioni sul nostro prossimo libro e sulle prossime produzioni cinematografiche potete visitare il nostro sito internet .

Op onze laatste pagina schittert de legendarische Mr. Jim Bailey. Jim heeft in Albert Hall opgetreden voor de Britse Koninklijke familie, en heeft meer dan 70 TV en film-optredens op zijn conto (inclusief mijn favoriet, The Carol Burnett Show).

We zijn zeer vereerd dat hij ons zijn medewerking heeft toegezegd.

We hopen dat u ervan genoten heeft de wereld van drag door onze ogen te zien. Het was een eer om hem aan u te mogen voorstellen.

Het boek dr.a.g. werd samengesteld om fondsen te werven voor onafhankelijke filmproducties. Alle performers en fotografen die aan bod komen, hebben hun werk, talent en beelden gratis ter beschikking gesteld, en daarvoor zijn we hen eeuwig dankbaar.

We hopen dat u een momentje neemt om deze performers en fotografen op te zoeken om te zien waar en wanneer u ze in actie kan zien. In deze moderne internettijden, volstaat een snelle online search om hun wereld te onthullen.

Neem een kijkje op onze website voor meer informatie over toekomstige boek- en filmproducties.

Christopher Logan
bookthefilm.com